SPIRITUAL REGENERATION and ESTABLISHMENT

The Long and Short Way to Conscious Union with Spirit

The serious seeker of Truth must continuously, consciously entertain in awareness, through devotion and dedication—even unto the last earthly breath if need be—this simple question:

What is God?

all the while *listening* for a response. This, in time, will cause the love gates to the inner Self to open, releasing that most wonderful still, small Voice.

—John F. Drewery Sr

SPIRITUAL REGENERATION and ESTABLISHMENT

The Long and Short Way
to Conscious Union
with Spirit

John F. Drewery Sr

Spiritual Regeneration and Establishment

The Long and Short Way
to Conscious Union with Spirit

John F. Drewery Sr

ISBN-13: 978-0692664100
ISBN-10: 0692664106
First edition 2016
Published by John F. Drewery Sr

For information contact:
johndrewery@yahoo.com
www.instillness.com

Cover photo by James Folley
Printed by CreateSpace
Available at Amazon.com

꙰ ꙮ

CONTENTS

Note to the Reader 7

Introduction 9

The Problem.. 15
Chapter 1
   The Cause 17

Chapter 2
   It's Impersonal 27

Chapter 3
   Absence of Spiritual Vision 37

The Effect.. 43
Chapter 4
   Acceptance of an Erroneous Belief 45

Chapter 5
   A Sense of Separation; Duality; Mortality.......... 50

Chapter 6
   Inharmony; Unhappiness 62

The Solution 71
Chapter 7
   For Those Who Missed the Way: The Spiritual
      Path Is the Way of Regeneration 73

Chapter 8
   Meditation Is a Necessity 80

Chapter 9
   Our True Self Must Be Experienced.................... 85

Chapter 10
   For Coming Generations: The Opportunity to
   Retain the Conscious Awareness of
   the Gift of Spirit 89

Chapter 11
   Original Perfection: Invisible Formlessness—
   Oneness.. 95

About the Author..107

Note to the Reader

The word *Consciousness* is a synonym for God; thus, in reverence, it is capitalized throughout the book.

The following words are defined relative to their use in the book.

Belief (noun): something believed; an opinion or conviction; confidence in the truth or existence of something not immediately susceptible to rigorous proof.

Believe (verb): to have confidence in the truth, the existence, or the reliability of something, although without absolute proof that one is right in doing so; to suppose or assume.

Cause (noun): a person or thing that acts, happens, or exists in such a way that some specific thing happens as a result; the producer of an effect.

Cause (verb): to bring into existence; to bring about; to produce.

Create: to cause to come into being as something unique that would not naturally evolve or that is not made by ordinary processes.

Form: something that gives or determines shape; a mold; external appearance.

Mortality: the condition or state of being subject to death.

Real: true; not merely ostensible, nominal, or apparent.

Sense: a feeling or perception produced through the organs of touch, taste, etc., or resulting from a particular condition of Consciousness.

Introduction

It was the message of The Infinite Way that flowed forth through Joel S. Goldsmith that first brought to my attention the notion of *the acceptance of belief*. Joel's message concerning belief was centered on the specific belief in two powers, but what seemed to grab me was simply the idea itself of accepting a belief. Belief is that which is *perceived through the senses* to be real or true. In other words, belief is a sense-based perception of reality. This inevitably conjured up the never-answered question: *What is the origin of belief?*

Has this question ever surfaced in your thought? If so, have you attained a satisfactory answer to it? For those who, like myself at one time, consider themselves in the dark regarding how we come to accept a belief, it is the intent of this writing to shed some light—that is, some spiritual understanding—on this subject as it pertains to our spiritual development.

From the very moment Joel's statement about the acceptance of the *belief* in two powers registered in my awareness, the ceaseless inquiry of why/how it happened also registered there. It felt to me that an answer to my questioning would yield permanent inner peace regarding the matter. It remained merely a feeling until, after many years of inward seeking, prolonged inward listening—meditation—the answer was revealed and the sought-after inner peace became a reality.

Universally, we have not individually had—nor do the vast majority of us presently have—conscious access to the spiritual Truth of our Being, even though, *in reality*, It is the very substance of what we truly are. The absence of this conscious access to the Truth has resulted in our *believing* that we are *in reality* material/physical bodies living in a material/physical world, whereas nothing could be further from the Truth.

Each of us possesses a physical body with which to express ourself on the material plane. We don't deny the existence of our physical body. But our only responsibility regarding the physical body is to knowledgeably understand and care for it. We are not to be overly concerned and attached to our physical body.

However, due to the universal lack of awareness, along with the teaching that our physical form is an illusion, no attention has been given to acquiring an understanding of the fact that universally our physical body does have a decisive *influence* upon the development of the ultimate state, spiritual or not, of our individual Consciousness.

The cloud of material belief that is accepted in individual Consciousness creates our individual material/human state of Consciousness. This state then becomes the cause, or source, of our material sense of the universe. The material state of Consciousness in the individual is what constitutes the inner blockage that prevents conscious access to the spiritual Truth, *the still, small Voice*—the most vital and necessary facet of our infinite, immortal, invisible nature because It is the *Spiritual Interpreter* of *everything* our individual Consciousness will become aware of. With conscious access to this *necessity (the still, small Voice)* being blocked, it's like the all-powerful sun in the sky—which does nothing but give forth light and warmth to the universe—being blocked by some meandering clouds that have drifted in front of it. What's more, the blockage will continue until the clouds are removed.

Material belief taints, defiles, darkens, and shutters the windows of the Soul from access to the Truth to such a complete extent that it causes us to erroneously perceive ourselves as physical/human beings, separate from all the other physical/human beings we see, and to behold the entire universe as a physical/material concept. Like the cloud-blocked sun, this state of Consciousness will remain intact until the false state is sufficiently dissolved to allow conscious access to the spiritual Truth that will eventually regenerate our original, true state of spiritual Consciousness.

As no spiritual revelation is a personal possession, even though it has to come forth in, through, and as the awareness of some specific person/individual, so this that has been spiritually revealed in me is being permitted to flow forth to the conscious awareness of any individual anywhere, whose Consciousness is prepared to receive it. This is a stupendous, eyebrow-raising revelation in that it has in it the potential to transform what we now universally know as human civilization into that of *spiritual civilization, spiritual realization*—heaven here on earth—for future generations.

There is much intellectual, historical material publicly available today, in various sources, on the past lives of the world's great saints, seers, and mystics, and for this reason, I will not devote additional time to such matters. Joel Goldsmith's voluminous writings are the ideal resource for anyone still needing to know or simply interested in such historical events and personages.

I want to get to the point now and deal with the matter at hand: what is the problem—and most importantly—what, if anything, can be done about it. In other words, what is the solution?

The problem and its solution understood spiritually (spiritually discerned) and *practiced,* acted upon, will in time universally elevate individual Consciousness to Its rightful spiritual state. Simply understanding the problem intellectually will not make a difference because this is not what will result in the needed *change of Consciousness*. Only the individual's *actual conscious contact* with the presence of the Spirit within will usher in that needed change of Consciousness.

Spiritual discernment, an outgrowth of this contact and a faculty of spiritual Consciousness, will make it possible for the Light of spiritual understanding to shine in individual you, me, and everyone. This faculty will reveal things to us that seem to be utter foolishness to our human sense. So be patient until you yourself make that inner, conscious contact with Spirit, because It will be that which reveals to you the truth—or not—of what has unfolded in and through me.

The Problem

The Problem

Chapter 1

The Cause

In spite of the tremendous strides in spiritual understanding that have been the fruitage of the world's metaphysical and spiritual teachings, the problem that the world continues to face is the universal spiritual ignorance of the role or influence of man's finite physical body in altering his original, pure, infinite, spiritual state of Divine Consciousness. However, the world is currently at the crossroads of being introduced to the cause of its predicament. It's anybody's guess just how long it will take for the world to accept what is about to be revealed.

Divine Consciousness is the infinite, omniscient, omnipresent, omniactive, causative Power and Principle of the universe, that which is symbolized by the biblical Garden of Eden. It is eternal, never having had a beginning, nor will It ever end. Divine Consciousness is One; thus, in spiritual reality, It constitutes the Source or Substance of the universe. The one Divine Consciousness, therefore, is the Source or Substance that is expressed individually as the Consciousness of man.

The symbology of Divine Consciousness as a garden is very appropriate. A garden itself actually symbolizes the aliveness of the earth in general. At no point is the earth anything but the earth. Although man has come to alter its inborn productivity by constructing buildings and all sorts of things that appeal to the human emotions, still, the nature of the earth is unchanged. But where the earth has remained unhampered and is free to be itself, a producer, it always does just that. Not only this—the earth performs its function of producing irrespective of what is permitted to find entry upon it. In other words, the earth will produce a beautiful flower and a poisonous hemlock side by side.

Consciousness is the spiritual, causative principle of life. It, too, performs Its function irrespective of what It becomes conscious of. In other words, It is impersonal. So that if *initially* It is aware of Its own nature as spiritual Truth, then absolute harmony will be established due to Its being *One*—Infinite. On the other hand, if Consciousness is *initially* exposed to the world of material appearances, due to lack of awareness (ignorance), then an erroneous material sense of existence, with all of the accompanying discord of humanhood, is produced.

Divine Individual Consciousness in man causes, or produces, the perception of reality/truth in whatever It is constantly, consciously aware of. This perception becomes the foundation of the individual's perspective of his world. If the substance of awareness in individual Consciousness is the experience of spiritual Truth, this Truth will be spiritually discerned as the reality of the universe and will manifest as love, joy, harmony, and goodwill among mankind universally.

On the other hand, if, as has been the case with mankind from time immemorial, individual Consciousness is aware of only material/physical forms or appearances, then a material sense of the universe will be accepted (believed) as reality and will manifest as all we know humanhood to be. In other words, individual Consciousness causes, or produces, the perception of reality/truth in whatever It is constantly, consciously aware of, *without exception*, and without regard as to whether it is in fact true or false.

It is *extremely important* for us to realize (understand clearly and fully) that Divine Consciousness is *omniactive*—that is, *always* functioning in, through, and as each individual one of us, from our very beginning. Symbolically, It is similar to the sun. The sun does nothing but shine, does nothing but spread light and warmth, because that is its function. Just because the sun is not visible where we happen to be at the moment doesn't mean that it isn't shining someplace in the world.

From the day we are born, Divine Consciousness, the one Consciousness that equally indwells everyone, causes the perception of reality/truth (belief) in anything—spiritual or material—of which It is constantly, consciously aware. It does this by Its ceaseless recognition, "*I AM*"—the identification of Itself *as* that very object of Its awareness. This is Its function.

Our own individual Consciousness is the garden that produces the fruitage of our individual experience. Consciousness is eternally functioning this way in, through, and *as* us individually, *whether or not* we are consciously aware of Its operation. Consciousness is the eternal Life and Power of our individual being. However, spiritual ignorance of the nature of the eternal operation of our omniactive Divine Consciousness, along with how to align ourselves with It, is what causes us to be living out from the erroneous human/material state of Consciousness rather than from the pure, spiritual state of Consciousness that is our true identity.

It is the function of Divine Consciousness, in man, to cause the perception of reality—the truth. Divine Consciousness, in Its changeless nature, always remains what It is—the impersonal, spiritual Truth of Being—"*I AM.*" It does not assume a different nature simply because mankind is spiritually ignorant of Its existence and the manner of Its operation, just as the sun remains what it is, whether or not it's visible, and the garden produces whatever seed comes to rest in it.

Spiritual ignorance of the fact that Divine Consciousness is fully operative—constantly and continuously proclaiming, "*I AM*" about anything It is aware of, regardless of whether it's actually true/real or not, and not knowing what to do to assure that Consciousness is only aware of the truth of Being—is the cause of the universal development in individual Consciousness of the belief in a material, or human, sense of existence.

Again, Divine Consciousness is *eternal*; that is, It has always existed, exists now, and will exist forever. It is perpetual, enduring, and changeless. Its nature is omnipotence, omnipresence, and omniscience: the Truth—that is, the still, small Voice, "*I AM*," which is the *Spiritual Interpreter*.

Divine Consciousness is perfect, complete, whole—One. Hence, It is *fully developed and eternally functioning*. Being One, It is the *Source* of everything; therefore, It is expressed, or made manifest, in infinite variety as the entire universe, which means It is expressed as the individual Consciousness of you, me, all mankind, and everything else. Its instrument and avenues of awareness—mind and the senses—likewise are *fully developed and eternally functioning*.

The question naturally arises: since Divine Consciousness Itself, the one Source, or Cause, is wholly perfect, why isn't this perfection reflected in and as the experience of Its individualized image and likeness—man?

This revelation was given to me, an instrument through which it might be allowed entry into human Consciousness, to be shared with the world of those who are receptive to it. As this is Truth being revealed in Consciousness, it can never afterwards go away. It will forever remain in human Consciousness, awaiting an individual here and an individual there to demonstrate it by firsthand experience.

This is what has been revealed to me. Although Consciousness Itself is always perfect and fully developed, the single most important facet of the nature of Divine Consciousness, omniscience (spiritual Truth)—which is comprised of the faculties of spiritual vision and spiritual discernment and whose constant presence is an absolute necessity in order to maintain Its own spiritual integrity—is *inaccessible* to Its individualized image and likeness (you, me, and everyone) in the very beginning—that is, at birth.

The reason for this lack of access is that when we take on a physical body, the location in that body from which Divine Consciousness is to function, the *"seat of Consciousness," is not sufficiently developed or evolved* to the stage where it is capable of admitting the spiritual Truth into the conscious awareness of the individual. The *seat of Consciousness* in the physical body is a portion of the brain known as the *frontal lobe*. This is the place of administration, *the seat of individual Self-Awareness.* Once sufficiently developed, it is the avenue through which spiritual Truth—the still, small Voice—declares Itself as *"I," "I AM,"* and is thereby experienced in our individual conscious awareness.

However, the difficulty is that this specific portion of the brain, although it is in the process of developing, is not *sufficiently developed* when we are born. This insufficient development is in keeping with its finite material nature. The field of neuroscience has revealed that the *frontal lobe* of the brain *does not become fully developed* until the individual reaches the late 30s to early 40s.

But all during this beginning stage, while there is insufficient development of the frontal lobe, our fully developed Consciousness is actively operating, thus causing a perception of reality (belief) in whatever It is constantly, consciously aware of through Its fully developed avenues of awareness, the senses, especially the eyesight. The spiritual Truth, the "*I AM,*" is a vital necessity to have consciously present in our individual Consciousness at all times because It *spiritually interprets* every form that our eyes behold. In Its absence, Consciousness perceives the ever-present world of material form (error) to be reality, the truth of being.

Remember, however, that even though *the seat of Consciousness* in the individual is not fully developed, this does not interfere with the operation of the law of Consciousness. Individual Consciousness Itself is nevertheless *always fully developed, fully conscious — proclaiming Its identity, "I AM,"* as every person, place, thing, or condition, and thus, always in operation. It causes, or produces, a perception of Reality in whatever is constantly, consciously perceived — Truth or error. Then Consciousness, as law, maintains and sustains that perception.

Since spiritual Truth is not a part of that awareness in individual Consciousness in the very beginning, the perception of reality is based solely on material appearances (forms)—something other than the spiritual Truth; in other words, error or falsehood.

Therefore, without exception, in the absence of the spiritual vision/interpretation provided by the spiritual Truth (the still, small Voice) that sees through material appearances to the spiritual reality, individual Consciousness causes, or produces, a false, material sense of the universe as reality.

This operation of the causative principle of Consciousness is instantaneously initiated universally in individual Consciousness *once the physical eyes are opened* following birth; it continues thereafter when the eyes are open, until the individual becomes aware of his own Self as *"I."* Unfortunately, by the time this Self-awareness enters, the perception of reality (belief) in a material sense of existence has already been accepted in individual Consciousness, and thus, the *"I,"* when It does become consciously known to the individual, interprets Itself, through that realized *material sense of existence,* to be the material body since that's all It has been aware of in regard to Itself.

Along with acceptance of the belief that the physical body is our true Self, our reality, all of the pleasurable (good) and painful (evil) conditions that we directly experience (now perceiving ourselves as the physical body) act to condition our Consciousness to accept the false belief in two powers, good and evil.

From the very beginning in man, individual Consciousness—*Omnipotence, the causative Principle*—

is unguided, undirected, uninstructed, unregulated, as the result of not having conscious access to spiritual Truth. This is due to the insufficiently developed state of the *"seat"* (organ) in the physical body of man from which Consciousness functions as the source of animation/life in a unique, individual manner. When that *seat of Consciousness* becomes sufficiently (not totally) developed, the individual is said to be self-aware as *"I."*

Neuroscience has established that this initial period of development of the frontal lobe *(seat of Consciousness)* takes anywhere from 24 to 36 months. Just imagine—pure, divine, individual Consciousness is being exposed to nothing but materiality for 24 to 36 months every moment the eyes are opened, at the very time (birth and thereafter) when It is the most susceptible to impression. There being no other awareness, of either knowledge or evidence, to stand as a nullification or contradiction to what It is perceiving, It accepts what It is aware of—the evidence of the physically conditioned senses, material appearances—as reality, which in turn causes the belief in the sense of a material universe. And from this belief, albeit an erroneous one, mind *forms* concepts that become the substance of the mental images of our world that we accept as the truth of being. This, a material sense of the world, is the world into which we are inducted when, later on, we become self-aware as *"I."*

God, the Christ in individual man, is *this very instant in reality*—that is, in the invisible—Omniscience. It is omnipresent throughout the universe, recognizing (spiritually loving) each and every person, place, or thing, without exception, as the expression of Itself. And It can do likewise *in this visible world of mankind,* if only you and I and everyone individually will permit It to do so by opening our own individual Consciousness for It to enter in.

However, there is no need for us to become impatient with ourselves, because this is not something that can be done humanly. It is the reason why we are on the spiritual path. Each one of us who has been led to this path is being drawn to Spirit by Spirit, and as we follow Its leading, It will lovingly bring us to that point where we become consciously aware of Its presence within us. This is all something that the indwelling Spirit in us accomplishes for Itself; it has nothing to do with you and me.

Chapter 2

It's Impersonal

Although we have accepted the *belief* that we are personally responsible for all that has befallen us—the good and not so good—we have yet to find the reason for having accepted such a *belief*. The truth is that none of this has been of our own personal doing. It is strictly impersonal. It is the normal, natural effect of the presence of the false material state of Consciousness; the state which maintains and sustains the *belief* in a *material sense* of self that is separate and apart from Spirit, the one true Self. While this state of Consciousness persists, the good and not-so-good conditions attending it will continue.

Many of us never question the value or significance of what has historically transpired in and as our human sense of life. That is, we rarely reflect on the times we were contented and wonder what happened to change them, and just how often this has been the case throughout our life.

We seldom pose the question, "Why?" We don't seem to see that no matter how much good we have experienced, it never lasted very long. It's as though we have become so accustomed to this on-again off-again happenstance of the good and not so good that it is mostly taken for granted and left there. The acceptance of such an attitude is a clear indication that we have not yet reached the point of disillusionment with the human way of life wherein we find ourselves pondering such questions as: Is this all there is to life? Is there no lasting peace to be experienced? What is the purpose of life? Why am I a part of it?

It is such probing and questioning of the invisible, nonmaterial issues of life as we humanly understand them—within ourselves, in secrecy, while telling no one else about what we're doing—that starts us on the way to the solution.

This that I am saying sounds all too familiar, I know—like so much of the seemingly garbled language of those possessing a knowledge higher than mere intellectual awareness. However, the unfamiliarity, contrary to what you may be thinking, is a plus because, if for no other reason, it is a reminder that there is a realm of life totally unknown to us. This aspect alone should be enough to propel us forward and perhaps ultimately onto the path of discovering something of this heretofore unknown realm.

Recall from Scripture that the things of Spirit are foolishness to the natural man, the human being— that is, man in his unillumined state. But it must be considered that all of the intellectual knowledge accumulated worldwide, down through the ages, hasn't done much to alleviate those issues of human living that so plague us moment by moment. In light of this, perhaps it wouldn't do us any harm, maybe even some good, to look further into some of this seemingly unintelligible information.

I say "seemingly" because that's the way it will first appear to anyone who delves into this arena with nothing more that the human intellect. As we gradually become enlightened on the subject of the spiritual realm, we will begin to perceive with greater understanding than when we were ignorant of such things.

It's worth repeating, to be clear we understand it, that all that has occurred and is still occurring in and as our human experience is not personal to you, me, or anyone else. This is true not only of the not so good but of the good as well. We are to take no personal credit or assume any responsibility for either. Any good we have done has been the spirit of God flowing through us as a blessing. Whether the good we have done has been for family, friend, or neighbor, it has had its source in the Spirit that animates us. Therefore, there isn't any justification for you and me to think that we ourselves are good. Instead, we are to view ourselves as instruments of Spirit.

On the other hand, neither are we to condemn ourselves as being evil because of any not-so-good acts we may have committed. The true cause of any such acts being done by us is the false state of Consciousness, the material state, which has developed in us. Due to its presence in our Consciousness, this false state is being maintained and sustained there by the law of Consciousness. Consequently, it will continue being present and causing inharmony until there is a change of Consciousness. Since Consciousness is One, It is based, or established, either in the spiritual Truth or, in the absence of that Truth, in error/falsehood.

Other than the fact that we are ignorant of the cause of our predicament, the rest — that is, the real reason behind it — is strictly impersonal. In Truth, in Reality, there is only *one* Person, or Presence, and that is Spirit. We have no life of our own, nor do we possess power to cause anything. You, I, everyone, and everything are nothing more than that one Spirit individually expressed or manifested. Our true nature, then, is the same as that of our Source. Since Spirit is infinite, there is no such thing as Spirit *and* something else. There is no you, me, *and* Spirit!

Spirit constitutes all there is to us. It is one perfect whole, manifested or expressed individually in infinite form and variety — but always One!

The great difficulty in this, however, is that these are true statements concerning things which are incomprehensible to the intellect. As a result, having only the intellect, we can certainly doubt them. But we can't agree with them because that requires spiritual understanding, something the human mind does not possess. We can only hang in limbo, so to speak, regarding these claims. But since it's clear that there is a realm of knowledge unknown to us — yet known to some — if we are intrigued enough to want to learn of this seemingly hidden knowledge, we will continue our journey on the spiritual path; for if followed with dedication and devotion, simply for the sake of *becoming aware of the spiritual Truth* and not for what we can get from It or how we can use It, then the door leading to the inner kingdom will surely open unto us.

The idea that you and I are living a life that we personally have not been responsible for—whether the experience has been fulfilling to some degree or totally devastating—is difficult to fathom. And this mystery is all the more reason to want to know what really is behind it all.

Deep within everyone is a sense that there is something we don't know, something about ourselves that is hidden from us. The *dark unknown* we face when closing our eyes elicits fright beyond measure, but with it is an intrigue, a mystery perhaps, since whatever that dark unknown is, it hasn't overtaken us or in any wise harmed us. Could it be that there is more to what lies hidden from us than we can at the moment imagine? Maybe there's nothing there at all to be frightened about; rather, some great good is lying dormant inside that darkened segment of us, and simply because we've not had the courage to investigate it in any depth, just the sheer unknown is what lies back of our dread.

We are made in the image and likeness of Spirit, but what we've known of ourselves up to this point certainly does not bear witness to that scriptural depiction. All that we have been involved in over the course of our lives, the good and not so good, has occurred in our experience because we have not been consciously in contact with the reality, that is, our true identity.

Had we been so connected, none of the good or not-so-good human issues could have taken place. The very nature of our being, as children of Spirit, would have been the animating power in our Consciousness. That power is Love. Had you and I individually, in our true identity, been in command, nothing but the spiritual harmony, peace, joy, cooperation, and love embodied within us would have been shown forth as our experience. But since this has not been the scenario of our lives, but quite the opposite, something else must have been, and still is, operating in us to cause it; and this is proof that whatever it is, is impersonal, having nothing at all to do with you and me individually.

In trying to get a mental glimpse of that which cannot be discerned by the human mind, it would do well to consider a garden. What we're really referring to here is getting a mental glimpse of the operation of Consciousness. So imagine a garden, if you will. We're also trying to get a glimpse of the impersonal nature of Consciousness and Its operation. Just think of a garden and how irrespective it is of whatever seeds are planted in it. The garden doesn't have anything to do with the choice of what it will bring into manifestation. Whatever the owner of the garden decides to plant, the garden will act, irrespective of the nature of the seed. It could be the seed of a poisonous plant, something that would harm anyone that eats the fruit of it; it could be a seed of some beautiful flower that would give pleasure to all those who are appreciative of beauty and of flowers of its nature; maybe even the seed of some luscious fruit or any other thing.

The point is that the garden itself makes no distinction; it will bring forth into existence, as fruitage, whatever is planted there. If the planter is ignorant of the types of seeds that are placed there — if, for instance, he or she happens to plant seeds of vegetation that are harmful to animals or people — the garden will bring forth that nature of fruitage.

This is similar to the way our Consciousness functions. It is fully operational at all times; in other words, Consciousness is constantly aware of something by virtue of Its avenues of awareness. If, from the very beginning, Consciousness has not been aware of the truth of Its own spiritual nature, Its own pure, spiritual Being (as has been the universal experience throughout history) then It brings forth, or manifests, something other than the Truth of Being.

Up to now, what is happening, strictly by virtue of spiritual ignorance alone, is that individual Consciousness, while being at the point of Its utmost purity — that is, in the very beginning — is *first* being exposed to nothing but appearances. And individual Consciousness, just like the garden, being continually exposed to these seeds/evidences of materiality, produces or causes corresponding life experiences.

This is how we come to have a material sense of the universe; the Truth of Being—the still, small Voice—is within individual Consciousness all the while, but It is inaccessible to the conscious awareness of the individual. And as has been the case, you and I individually—those of us who in previous incarnations have had our fill of the human sense of life—have come to the point where we are ready to dive within ourselves to get some answers to our many questions about some permanency to the life experiences of peace, joy, and harmony. We want to find out how we can possess these types of things and not have to go back and forth between having and not having them. In other words, we want to make them permanent.

In order for that to be true in your life and in mine, we have to come to understand this impersonal nature of Consciousness, or Spirit, and realize that ultimately *something takes form, something results* any time we are conscious, even while we are ignorant of the operation of our own Consciousness, and we must understand what needs to be done in order to assure that the spiritual Truth is the only knowledge to which our Consciousness is *first* exposed.

Because mankind, as a whole, has been and continues to be ignorant of the impersonal problem, there has been no effort to rectify it. As long as the impersonal problem remains unknown to man, there can be no change. Change will come only as man becomes consciously aware of what the problem is and goes within himself—turns within and seeks a solution. The solution is there and always has been, but until an individual here and there becomes aware of that solution, it's as if it doesn't exist.

Those of us on a spiritual path have been called that we may become instruments through which the Light of Spirit—that inner Light, that Light which mankind as a whole is unaware of—can enter human Consciousness and effect the needed change. When we come to understand this, we will see the crucial role that we are given; a role which has the potential of affecting the affairs/life experience of future generations. Of course, in the process it will affect our own affairs, but what is more important is that a start be made so that it can ultimately evolve into a way of life which bestows a blessing upon mankind universally.

This is something that will be evolutionary; it won't take place overnight, as we would humanly prefer. It's just like any other new practice or knowledge that man comes to possess. First, he has to absorb it intellectually; once understood, it must be practiced in everyday living so that it becomes established in Consciousness. This is the way of Consciousness. There is no way man can learn something intellectually and through some miracle put it to immediate use.

What a burden is lifted from the shoulders. How liberating it is to know that you and I have not been in the past, nor are we presently, personally responsible for the human conditions in our lives. All of this is attributable to our lack of spiritual awareness. But from where we are presently, we must go on to learn the cause of our situation and, more significantly, how it happens to be such that it is and what, if anything, can be done about it. Because as long as the cause of our problem and the reason for it is unknown to us, we have no guarantee that it won't reoccur once the issue is outwardly resolved. We want to discover the way to eliminate the cause of the problems permanently.

This can be done only by seeking the solution from the infinite Source of intelligence that is found only within individual you and me. When we can consciously accept the truth that the kingdom of God is within us and that everything we could possibly need is there, including the solution to any human problem, we will readily turn away from our human intellect to this infinite Source within us.

Chapter 3

Absence of Spiritual Vision

What, then, is the cause of our *seeming* to be physical/human beings? It is the fact that from the very beginning we are not aware of the spiritual Truth of our being. In other words, each individual, when born, is devoid of access to the most important facet of his true nature—*spiritual vision*. Instead, because of lack of awareness, ignorance really, our Consciousness is permitted to be exposed to the world of material appearances which, in the absence of any changeless, contradictory knowledge, It readily accepts as the truth or reality of being.

We have learned from the experience of the world's illumined souls, those individuals with some degree of spiritual vision, that we have accepted an illusory world, which includes ourselves, as the truth or reality of Being. But none of those illumined ones of which I am aware have, for me at least, satisfactorily explained just how we came to accept such a belief.

Viewed from the standpoint of spiritual Truth, the entire mortal, material scene is an illusion. This, however, is not a denial of the existence of the material picture; it is simply the acknowledgment that what we have beheld of the world through the avenues of sense is not the spiritual Truth. This is the perspective of those among us who have been blessed with spiritual vision and spiritual discernment. To all others, the material picture is quite real since they have not been made aware of anything other than what they are able to know with the physical senses, and that is material appearances. But the things of Spirit cannot be perceived this way. To be able to discern the spiritual Truth of existence requires the development of the spiritual faculties. This implies that these are potentially available to everyone.

It must be thoroughly understood—realized—that Divine Individual Consciousness, your Consciousness and mine, is forever the cause, or producer, of our perception of reality, our belief. That's all a belief is—an interpretation or perception of reality in whatever Consciousness is conscious of. And once the belief is accepted in Consciousness—whether it's the Truth or, in Its absence, falsehood/error—that belief is then maintained and sustained by the law of Consciousness until there is a change of Consciousness.

Fortunate is the individual who has broken through the false belief in the reality of mortal existence to discover that he or she, as well as everyone else, possesses a spiritual nature that is infinite, immortal, invisible, and eternal. This individual lives in a different world than the majority of mankind. This individual knows, and is thus living, the meaning of "My peace," that peace which only the true "*I*" of us exudes.

From time immemorial, the study and research of the spiritual way of life has centered itself exclusively in the various scriptures and recorded spiritual revelations of the world. Each of these, in its own manner of expression, has propounded the truth of the existence of the one *infinite* spiritual Self. But to my knowledge, none of them has considered what influence or impact, if any, the *limited* material form — in, through, and as which Spirit is individually manifested or expressed — may exert.

It is inconceivable that the *infinite* Spirit could be present or expressed in a *limited* environment (a material/physical body) with no restrictive consequences. The allness of Infinite Consciousness, or Spirit, cannot possibly be fully manifested unless It remains pure, absolutely unrestricted — free of exposure to appearances — in the very beginning. Therefore, *first* allow Spirit to establish Itself as a realized state in the conscious awareness of the individual, and It will forever after be that changeless Omnipresence that will spiritually interpret, through spiritual vision, all that will ultimately constitute the individual's world. The individual, in other words, will then be anchored in his real identity — spiritual Consciousness, Truth — his original, spiritual heritage.

The limited physical form (the body) that Divine Consciousness uses as an instrument through which to express Itself is insufficiently developed at birth.

As a result, Divine Consciousness is left aware solely of the world of appearances. The Truth is not available to It! Divine Consciousness does not have access to Its own omniscience at this time — at the birth of the individual. This is because the place/location/seat in the body (physical form) from which our fully active and developed Divine Consciousness is to operate is in the very early stage of development. This renders it incapable of admitting our essential spiritual vision and discernment of the spiritual Truth from the very beginning.

Nevertheless, with the *opening of the eyes* (physical eyesight), our fully developed Consciousness, in the absence of spiritual vision, is *instantly exposed* to the world of appearances. From then on, It is constantly and continuously exposed to them, and in accord with the law of Its creative nature, It instantly goes about accepting what It is aware of as Reality, thereby creating the belief to that affect.

It will be in the following months, when our physical development has become sufficient to admit entry of the Self, the *"I,"* into conscious awareness, that It (the *"I,"* the Interpreter) will interpret Itself in terms of the material/physical sense that has already been accepted as Reality. Therefore, the *"I"* accepts Its material/physical form as Its Reality.

The limited, material sense of existence develops from the limited perception of the eyesight (physical vision). If the Truth of Being is to be revealed, it will have to be done through the development of the

faculty of spiritual vision, a faculty that very few consciously possess even in this age of enlightened Consciousness, in spite of the truth that each of us already possesses this faculty. It's just that we are not conscious of it.

How, then, do we become aware of it? The secret to the development of spiritual vision is the same as the secret to the whole spiritual way of life: making a conscious contact with our true spiritual Self—our real Identity. Again and again, the Master's directive that "the kingdom of God is within you" comes to the forefront of our awareness. When will you and I cease our seeking and searching in the external, where Spirit is nowhere to be found, and wholeheartedly turn our attention instead to discovering the vastness of our own Self? Whenever this singular motive of finding the Spirit within us, merely for the sake of the experience itself and for no other reason, has thoroughly engulfed us as the number one priority of our life, we will be prepared and ready for Its entry into our conscious awareness.

Spiritual vision is attained when Consciousness is exposed to formlessness—that is, to the Infinite Invisible. It simplifies matters if this is the *first* and *only* constant, conscious exposure that the individual Consciousness has, so that the spiritual Truth, "*I*," the "*I AM*," becomes accepted and is thereby active in and as the individual's conscious awareness. In this way, from the very beginning the individual is blessed with the conscious awareness of the Presence of the Spiritual Interpreter, the "*I AM*," which will forever after first—*first!*—reveal the spiritual, invisible, true nature of everything that will subsequently appear to the individual's physical eyesight. But from where we are now in conscious development, this is but the ideal, not the actuality.

Due to lack of awareness, whatever individual Consciousness is *first* exposed to now is, without exception, only this world of material forms— appearances. As a result, Consciousness quickly comes to accept materiality as the reality/truth of being as Its foundational belief. So that later on, when the spiritual Truth, "*I*," the "*I AM*," enters conscious awareness, It misinterprets Itself as being the physical form, the body, due to the erroneous foundational belief in the reality of material form that has been previously accepted.

The Effect
of the Problem

Introduction

The effect of the problem is twofold. First, there is the creation or acceptance of the belief in a physical/material sense of self that is separate and apart from the one spiritual Self; in other words, a belief in a false physical/material selfhood. Second, the outcome of this false belief is the acceptance of the two powers, good and evil. The seeming reality of these two powers initially develops from having experienced in the physical/material body both pleasure (good) and pain (evil) as interpreted by the previously accepted false sense of self.

Chapter 4

Acceptance of an Erroneous Belief

Although unknown to us at the time, by our acceptance in Consciousness of an erroneous belief about ourselves, we relinquish our spiritual heritage as sons of God—individualized expressions of Consciousness, Spirit—and instead become human beings.

Spirit/Consciousness is the *One* Reality comprising all that exists. In other words, It is God! Being *One*, It is infinite, whole, perfect, invisible, and immortal. Its nature is omnipotence, omnipresence, omniscience, and most notably, without question, eternally *conscious*.

The *One* Spirit/Consciousness is the infinite, invisible substance of the universe expressed in infinite form and variety, which includes Its own image and likeness—individual Consciousness (man)—that is, you, me, and everyone. Thus, contrary to all appearances, in Reality, taken as a whole, we individually constitute the very image and likeness of the *One* Spirit/Consciousness; therefore, in Reality, each of us is constituted of nothing except Its divine attributes and nature.

Unlike the *One* Source (Spirit, Consciousness), however, Its image and likeness (man, individual

Consciousness) comes possessed with an additional feature. It has a finite, physical form (material body) as Its means of individual expression on the material plane of existence. It is this limited form, or at least an aspect of it, that has a tremendous—though unrealized—*influence* on the state/condition that from the very outset inevitably develops universally in individual Consciousness.

This predicament will continue as long as this *influence* is not known and thereby left unaddressed. However, once its existence is detected, it can be regulated, if not completely eliminated, by being brought under the dominion of the Truth, which is an omnipresent quality of individual Consciousness.

From eternity, man has sought to understand the *reason* for the seeming separation between God and himself. He has sought in different ways to find an answer by realizing the nature of God and, on the other hand, by trying to learn something of his own nature. There is currently ample written and recorded knowledge regarding both the nature of God and man, and this is publicly available to anyone who is the least bit interested; therefore, I find no need to reiterate it here. But it is worthwhile to reiterate the fact that we, as humans, are such due to the acceptance in Consciousness of an erroneous belief about our true nature.

To my knowledge, no one with at least an intellectual awareness of the nature of God and man has ever looked beyond the familiar scriptural and psychological context of that relationship—not even for a clue. There has been no awareness of or credence given to any notion that an aspect of man's physical form plays a significant role in *influencing* the outcome of that relationship.

The Garden of Eden is symbolic of the *One* pure spiritual Consciousness, which includes Mind symbolized as Adam—the Intellect; Soul symbolized as Eve—the Feelings; and Body symbolized as both Adam and Eve—the Form. This is the original, universal, spiritual endowment or composition of Consciousness, individual Consciousness; that is, mankind—*Oneness.*

So how is it that man is *seemingly* separated from this spiritual Oneness? In order to understand this, it becomes necessary to understand the status of Consciousness when It individualizes as man—you and I.

A good place to begin is with the awareness that *even with the eyes closed* our individual Consciousness, which is Divine Consciousness—the omnipotent, creative Principle—is still active, still conscious. Being conscious is Its nature; hence, never is It anything but conscious. *Consciousness is never unconscious!* It is always conscious by way of the avenues of awareness, the senses.

In their original pure state, the senses are spiritual in nature. Vision (spiritual or physical) is the most significant and influential of the senses. Whatever the senses are constantly and continuously aware of—

spirituality or materiality—determines the ultimate "state" of the individual's Consciousness.

Man—individual Consciousness—from the very beginning has been exposed *first* to this world of material appearances. At no time during that period has any trace of the spiritual Truth been revealed, which, had it been consciously known, would contradict and thus nullify any materialistic claims and the effects that would otherwise result due to their acceptance.

As a result, man has found himself universally, although totally unaware of it, imprisoned in a material sense of life, which has caused him to identify his Being—his Self—as the physical/material body he has always seen and otherwise experienced through the physical senses. The total ignorance of the spiritual truth concerning his real identity—while being constantly and continuously exposed to nothing except material appearances through the senses, especially the eyesight, at the crucial beginning stage of individual existence—is the reason individual Consciousness, functioning naturally, normally, and impersonally, creates and accepts the belief in a material sense of self, a self that is separate from the one true spiritual Self.

Consciousness causes or creates our perceptions of Reality—that which, to the individual, is true. This Consciousness does in an impersonal or neutral manner, without any regard whatsoever as to whether or not Its perception is based on that which is actually true. Even if what It is perceiving is erroneous, Consciousness, in due time, will nevertheless cause/create and accept the belief that what is being perceived is true. In other words, it will be the truth of the matter insofar as the individual is concerned. This is the way Consciousness operates or functions—*this is the law of Consciousness.*

This law of Consciousness is eternally in operation; when Consciousness individualizes as you and I, It is fully operational from day one. However, this *day one*, as it relates to the creation of what is to be our individual life experience, is *the first day we open our eyes.* Our opened eyes initiate the operation of Consciousness in and as our very own individual life experience, whereby our sense (spiritual or material) of the world (the universe) is created, accepted (believed) and, as such, perceived as *Reality*—the truth.

Chapter 5

A Sense of Separation;
Duality; Mortality

The world was what it was in the past, is what it is today, and will be in the future: a world divided against itself. It's a world characterized by a universal sense of separation. This world of separated human beings will never be able to solve its problems for any length of time because there is no real spiritual Love there.

The only love that exists among human beings is the personal sense of love—love of self, family, and friends, which, in spiritual reality, is not Love at all. For with the personal sense of love, man does not include his fellow man. Spiritual Love is that Love which recognizes only spiritual identity; therefore, It perceives all as One.

There is, in spiritual reality, no separation. What we are dealing with is a *sense* of separation, and a *sense* of something develops from perceiving with only the senses. This universally being the case with mankind from the very beginning, we have come to accept ourselves, as well as everyone and everything else, as separate entities. This is not the Truth of Being. The Truth is oneness.

This world of separation will continue until such time as the universally prevailing erroneous sense of separation is nullified in individual Consciousness. Each individual is the vey image and likeness of Consciousness and therefore possesses the very nature of Consciousness. There is no other God or spirit that is going to be added to us. We're already infinite. So what lies ahead of us is our own individual responsibility. The nullification of the erroneous sense of separation will happen as the result of the realized, actually established, conscious Presence of the spiritual Truth of oneness in our individual Consciousness.

Unfortunately, this cannot be done collectively or universally. Going to church, classes, group gatherings won't do it because each of us is the individualized fullness of Consciousness/"I AM"/ Spirit/God, and as such, we are totally independent of one another. While we are separated, nothing taking place in the Consciousness of a person has any effect in the Consciousness of another.

This means that you and I individually, by our own work within our Consciousness, have to nullify the erroneous sense of separation. We have to learn the correct letter of truth to be used in our periods of contemplation; we must, in the everyday situations of our life, intellectually practice this truth we're learning so that it takes root in our Consciousness; and, above all, we are to use what we learn as an aid to quiet the thinking mind in preparation for the real phase of meditation—*expectantly listening* into the Silence.

This—individual responsibility—is the reason complete emancipation of the world at large is nowhere in the foreseeable future. Complete freedom will always be lurking in the background as a potentiality. But due to the fact that not everyone is developed in Consciousness to the point of being totally disenchanted with life as lived in this illusory human sense of existence, it will take untold future generations for mankind as a whole to be transformed in Consciousness if the task is left up to individuals.

This is not meant to cast a hopeless shadow upon the world, however, because it has been promised that "ten righteous men," that is, just a few persons who have actually realized the truth, can work wonders on a grand scale among men. This they do first among family, friends, and associates, then in their community, nation, and ultimately in the world. But as it now stands, realizing the Truth individually is the fate of those of us who missed out—due to lack of awareness—on the opportunity to be protected from the effects of allowing our Consciousness to be prematurely exposed to the material world.

We will first have to undergo the experience of living our lives as the human beings we believe ourselves to be. In this way, each one has to thoroughly exhaust himself humanly by going right ahead in the human effort to satisfy all the desired, imagined ways of attaining whatever is the human objective. And really, there is only one goal in the life of human you and me, and that is happiness and peace through fulfillment.

Some of us will go through many more human lifetimes before it finally dawns in us that no lasting contentment is to be found in the human world. It is only when we reach the stage of disenchantment or disillusion, by whatever means necessary in each individual life, that we will be prepared to seek within ourselves—the one place we have failed to investigate—for some solution to our human dilemma.

There are signs of a worldly nature that strides are being made to alter our sense of separation. One of these is the advent of satellite news. With news media companies having access to every corner of the universe, no longer is it possible for any country to plot against another in secret. What's going on in one country is immediately available via satellite news to every other country. And when there is some unrest taking place, the world is immediately aware of it and is therefore, if need be, able to take action that is in its own best interest. Nowadays, however, countries by and large are more reluctant to act as they once did—launching attacks, dropping bombs, sinking vessels—all because none of this, even in the preparatory stages, can go unnoticed by the rest of the world.

As barriers of living separately from each other, either as individuals or countries, are removed, it becomes easier for us to get along because we come to lose our ignorance and superstitions regarding one another. Instead, we come to know one another from our own experience instead of from the ignorance and superstitious beliefs passed from one generation to the next. As I get to know you, I make my own assessment of the type of person you are rather than base my judgment on something I may have read or heard about you.

Only through personal, firsthand interaction can this happen. Once we have become the least bit comfortable humanly with one another, we can go further and turn our attention inward to bring forth a deeper understanding of our relationship to each other.

The sense of separation causes us to lose the benefit of the free flow of Spirit because it personalizes and limits who is to be the recipient. We're only interested in benefitting those we consider close to us—family, friends, and associates. Then, too, when the sense of separation has dominion in our Consciousness, nothing is actually flowing from us but the desire to get, accomplish, or achieve something. Our whole focus is on increasing our lot. When this is the case, we shut off any outpouring of the Spirit through us; It remains dammed up.

The sense of separation serves no useful purpose. It only serves to perpetuate our morbid human condition. While this state of Consciousness persists in individual you and me, we can always expect to have the same conditions and circumstances in our life experience. It is only when we turn from our human sense of the world, turn within and make a consciously known contact with our true Self, with Spirit, that we begin opening out the way that permits the imprisoned splendor—our true identity—to escape into human Consciousness and be a blessing to anyone anywhere in the universe who is also seeking answers to the meaning of being alive.

Duality, the belief in good and evil, is another universally shared false belief that is a product of the sense of separation. The reason duality is universal is that, due to lack of awareness, each individual expression of Consciousness—you and I—undergoes the same experience right from the moment of birth. Just as Consciousness/God is the one creative principle and is therefore the creator and substance of the universe in all of Its infinite forms and varieties, in Its individualizations as mankind (as you and I), It is the creator and substance of our individual life experience. In other words, our Consciousness is the creative principle of our life experience. Since It is the very image and likeness of Divine Consciousness/God—Omnipresence, Omnipotence, Omniscience—Its true nature is Godlike, all good, Truth. How, then, in the midst of such allness and perfection, does the sense of good and evil develop?

The causative principle, or creative power, of Consciousness, individual Consciousness, commences producing the basic foundation of the life experience of the individual—the perception of that which is real, true—the instant the individual's eyes open. If the first thing consciously perceived is the spiritual Truth of Being, then the individual will be blessed with spiritual Consciousness. On the other hand, if the first conscious perception is of the material universe, then eventually the individual will be imprisoned in material Consciousness.

The individual's state of Consciousness—spiritual or material—begins taking form the instant the eyes open, but the individual is not as yet self-conscious; that is, not self-aware at this time. No matter—Consciousness, the Source of Being, in the individual is always aware, always conscious, always perceiving, recognizing, or interpreting whatever It is aware of as the reality, the Truth of Being, which is the truth about Itself.

By virtue of Its nature as law, whatever Consciousness is constantly, consciously aware of once the eyes are open becomes accepted as the reality of the life experience of that individual. Then everything concerning the individual is interpreted from the standpoint of this perception. Up to this present day, universally, when the individual's eyes are opened, Consciousness is constantly, consciously exposed to or aware of nothing but appearances, so that in every

56

individual a material sense of existence becomes accepted as real, true—reality, in other words.

Although this is the norm of the human sense of life, it is not the Truth of Being! Nevertheless, having been accepted in Consciousness as the belief about Being—Life/Existence—that erroneous belief becomes the basis or substance of the interpretation/perception of every aspect of the individual's life experience that is to follow.

Once self-awareness ("*I AM*") is attained, the first interpretation the individual will make is of the "*I*" that will utter Itself within him. When that "*I*" makes Itself known, Consciousness, having accepted the material appearance as the reality of the individual, will interpret Itself as the physical body. It does this through the medium of that accepted false material sense—so that I, the individual, am my physical body.

Along with this acceptance come the varied physical sensations experienced by the body. Some of these sensations are very pleasant—good; others are not at all pleasant—they're bad. All of this, remember, is taking place in the individual's Consciousness before he has become aware of himself as "*I*."

In spite of the fact that this early accepted false belief is not the Truth of Being, still it characterizes the universal state of Consciousness of mankind today. It is what it is because from the very beginning, Consciousness, once individualized as man, has no immediate, conscious access to the Truth of Its own Being. If from the very beginning It had access to the

Truth, then spiritual Truth would be accepted as the reality of Being, and as a result, it would become the changeless foundation and anchor of individual Consciousness. Its consciously known Presence Itself within the individual would make it impossible for any material or mental claim to impose itself upon the individual's Consciousness.

The destiny of a mortal is death. There isn't anyone who is not functioning from a material state of Consciousness (mortality) in some degree, some less so than others due to a higher measure of conscious preparation in previous life experiences. Nonetheless, all of us have this fear firmly established within our Consciousness because it is so very well known, from our viewing this world of appearances, that the ultimate end of physicality is the grave, which means extinction.

It is this fear of extinction that causes us to give undue concern to the physical body and its operation. This fear-based belief concerning the body is the cause of the discordant bodily health conditions that we so frequently experience.

All there is to mortality is Consciousness functioning in the absence of Truth. There really is but one true state of Consciousness—the spiritual state. But if this state is not permitted to be established in the individual from the very beginning, another state—a false state—will develop normally and naturally in its absence since Consciousness is impersonal, or neutral, having no special regard for anything to which It may be constantly and continuously exposed. This means Consciousness will perform unerringly, no matter the nature—truth or error—of what It is aware of.

In absence of the Truth of Being, Consciousness knows, or is aware of, nothing but the world of appearances in the external. For us individually, the important aspect of this perception is that it includes our physical, material appearance—the body—as the truth, or reality, of who or what we really are. This is an error! However, Consciousness does not dispute it but instead goes right ahead maintaining and sustaining that false notion, thereby causing it to be the foundation, or basis, of how we view our world. What we see through the eyesight is a material universe and that we are a lone, separate, mortal part of it.

Mortality, the acceptance of the belief in a self separate and apart from Spirit, a material sense of being that can get sick, diseased, aged, and die, is what generates all of the fear known by man. While we are in this state of Consciousness, fear will remain. It has to, because life seen as being constituted of materiality—the changeable—can have no other effect than eventual extinction. This is what is universally feared more than anything else.

If there were not the prospect of death lingering in the back of our thought, life would be a supreme joy every moment. We would take pleasure in all the people, places, things, and activities that make up our present experience. Never would we have to venture outside of what is ours in an effort to add some person, place, or thing to what is already present for us. Having no sense of fear, we would know that each succeeding moment would bring with it another joyful experience filled with all that is needed to make it a delight for all concerned.

If you and I had no sense of being physical bodies, we would rob death of its influence in our life. Our seeming mortality is the root of all fear! Take just about any fear you can think of and see if it doesn't relate to some imaginary circumstance involving something happening to our physical body—that is, what we believe to be the self. If something were to affect the body, it would, in effect, be affecting us. So if we catch a cold, it isn't the cold itself that gives us concern. No, it's what that cold could possibly do to the body if it isn't healed or cured. It's always how a circumstance will affect our body—better known humanly as our life—that overwhelms us with dread.

The belief that we are in reality our physical body is the cause of all this fear. As a matter of fact, it's the one cause behind all of our fear. For example, just walking down a street after dark gives just about everyone the jitters. Why? Is it the darkness or the particular street that is of concern? No, it's what might happen to us—the body—physically, from someone lurking in the shadows. That's our real concern. If we walked with the spiritual awareness of God/Consciousness as the infinite substance of the universe, then we would realize fully that nothing could possibly develop in our pathway but something Godlike. Even if someone did step out of, or appear in, the shadows, our spiritual sense would instantly let us know that this too is what *"I AM,"* so be still … be at peace … be not afraid … it is *"I."*

Chapter 6

Inharmony; Unhappiness

Look at your own life and ask yourself the question: Has there ever been a time when there was a span of harmony among your family, friends, and associates that lasted? You may find, as I have, that these instances of harmony were short-lived. Harmony did occur at times, but it never lasted. There always seemed to be something, if nothing but a difference of opinion, that ended the harmony. Granted, the harmony eventually was recaptured, but it wasn't long before some other issue cropped up to once again dispel the harmony.

There seems to be more of this among those we know well than among others we know. It seems that close associates like family and friends know that nothing can alter the fact of family or friendship, so we take liberties with one another much more readily than we do with those with whom we don't have a deep connection, those from whom we are seeking to get or acquire friendship.

As humans, the harmony of our life is dependent, it seems, on what we can get from others. As long as we can do this to our liking, our relationships are harmonious, at least to our own way of thinking. The other person, of course, has mostly the same outlook, so at some point the two will clash, thereby creating some friction. "Love you one another as I have loved you" is not addressed to a human being. It is addressed to the true identity, our true Self, giving It the direction for obtaining a harmonious life experience no matter who may constitute our relation—friend or foe.

Inharmony is the nature of human Consciousness. How could it possibly be otherwise since the human being is only out for himself. It appears to be him against the world since everything he desires is outside himself, and it's all left up to him to "get" from the world—in whatever way he can devise— those things that will satisfy him. Little does he realize that what he seeks is not going to fill that empty void in his soul. It takes something other than materiality to do that.

Nonetheless, we will never attain a sense of harmony out in the world of fleeting pleasures. Each material possession places its own demands on the individual. Sooner or later, these wear us down to the point where we see that the possession of an inordinate amount of material things such as money, land, houses, etc., only distances us further from ourselves, and this can only lead to internal inharmony. This is really where the inharmony takes its toll— within the Consciousness of the individual—for here it is that we are either at one with the indwelling Spirit, or we are a house divided against itself—a state of inharmony.

The only way we will be able to free ourselves from desire for the things out in this world, things that we believe will result in a harmonious life, is to prove it to ourselves by pursuing them. It won't do any good pretending that we don't desire money, health, reputation, position, etc. Our Consciousness will know better. We can't deceive the all-knowing Wisdom within us. Therefore, why try?

Go ahead and be, do, out in this world and see what it provides. Perhaps what it gives you, the individual, is sufficient for you at this stage of your development. If so, that's all well and good for you now. But for others, the realization may dawn during this life experience that nothing worldly can satisfy for any great length of time, certainly not permanently. These individuals will have come full circle to that place where they have had it with the temporary ups and downs of this human sense of life, and out of sheer desperation they will turn within with soul-searching questions flooding the attention — questions such as "What is God? What is Spirit? What is Consciousness? Is this all there is? Is there no peace on earth for man?"

The burden of expectations creates inharmony in our lives. The expectations that we place upon others and that others place upon us engender inharmony. Of course, as human beings, this is all we know to do — to "get," to always expect something to come to us from some source or from somebody else. While we continue to have expectations of others, there will always be a sense of burden or obligation, and such a sense will always lend itself to discord among human beings.

At no time do we as humans give thought to giving of ourselves without an expectation—giving out of the sense of wanting to share simply because the sharing itself produces an invisible gift within us and because the more we can experience this invisible gift the more we want to experience it. As we see that we are actually in control of that gift by our giving, by our sharing, then we will also naturally want to do more to have that gift come alive in us more often.

Do not be misled. Inharmony is not without a purpose. All those things that tend to keep us off balance, let's say, uncomfortable as human beings, are serving a purpose. They are pushing us to the limit, pushing us to do all the seeking and searching that we can in this human world so that we can get to that place where we are ready to open the door to that "I" that stands knocking within, to that spirit of God within us. It is waiting for us to become disenchanted and disillusioned with this life we have lived separate and apart from It so that we will then turn to the only place where the real answers to life's problems are found, the only place we have never, ever looked on our own: within ourselves.

Rightly understood, inharmony and many of the other problems we face as human beings are actually aids, helps, on the way; without them, we would not take a step, would not take any action, because as humans we so love our comfort and ease. And as long as we are in that state, we will do nothing. Oh, but let us be ill, uncomfortable, disturbed, fearful, impoverished, or lonely, and these things will move us to some type of action—move us to do something. In trying to remedy those problems, we will find ourselves being drawn nearer and nearer to that place where we shall be more than willing to open the door and admit that "I" that stands knocking.

The lack of awareness of our true spiritual identity renders us human beings, who cannot please Spirit and are not under the laws of Spirit. Could this possibly be the reason why there is no such thing as a happy human being? Unhappiness, on the whole, is man's lot in just about every avenue of life. It will remain that way because in that state we are forever looking for some thing or some person apart from us to fill the empty void we experience from waking to sleeping. The void cannot be filled by person, place, or thing. But since we know of no other way to fill it, we trudge right along.

There will come a time, however, when we weary of our human trek, and this uneasiness will prompt us to make a deeper search. It may very well take some of us still more lifetimes before we are totally put off by our humanhood. So many are still attached to human comfort and ease and are therefore not willing to relinquish these quite yet. Such individuals will have to pursue their journey spiritward at a much slower pace because they are likened to the "rich man" who had too many possessions. That is to say, they are still attached to things of one nature or another. Until you and I are able to loose things and people—not consider them all that important— we are attached to this material world and thus unable to enter the world of Spirit because any manner of attachment will block our entry.

The invisible Spirit is the substance of all that appears outwardly as effect. Thus, possessing the effects without their substance means that as these forms change or leave us, we are left unhappy. Our reliance was on the shadow that forever is here today and gone tomorrow rather than on the substance, reality, or cause.

All unhappiness stems
from being separated from Me.

Our entire human experience is spent attempting to achieve some measure of happiness. Every thing, person, place, or circumstance is sought with that objective in mind. It seems as though we can never find fulfillment, so we are constantly searching for it. We have to explore all the human or material prospects that come to us as ideas; otherwise, these will linger in the background of our mind, forever gnawing at us. This will give us no rest, so the best approach is to rid ourselves of them by going right ahead in pursuit of them. In this way, we will solve the problem of knowing if it will indeed content us;

if not, we can move to the next thing that crops up. The other problem that will be resolved by our pursuit of the objective is that it will give us a degree of temporary peace since we don't have to beat ourselves up with "What if ...?" regarding the objective.

Like all other discords associated with living as a human being, unhappiness is not a permanent dispensation. It can be overcome. But it does require each individual's heartfelt desire for happiness— that is, for the experience of the Spirit. This may often temporarily cause more unhappiness due to the changes that will be needed in order to leave the material realm of life and enter the spiritual realm.

Many cherished attachments will have to be released or loosed. These may include other people as well as things and circumstances. Most of us haven't a clue as to just how attached we are to this material world, and having to part with it can be quite a shock. But if we realize that there is an indescribable peace and contentment behind all the seeming turmoil initiated by our desire to seek something this world has to offer, this realization will spur us onward in spite of the difficulties of the moment.

Each of us has to unburden ourself of lifetimes of accumulated humanhood. That's what is going on when we "die daily." The process is so gradual that sometimes it lets us know very well that dying itself could not be too much worse than what we are going through on a daily basis.

Unfortunately, there is no one who can tell us just how long the spiritual journey back to the center of our being, to be restored to our true original identity, will take. Each one is a unique, individual manifestation with a different life experience. Some, in other lifetimes, have been more spiritually prepared than others, and these will progress further. But all of us are equally endowed of Spirit, so there is no need to feel downtrodden because of our own situation when we see one here and one there who is manifesting evidence that they are further along than we are. We must simply follow our own inner guidance or leading and trust It, as Omniscience, to know exactly what is needed for us to move ahead.

The Solution

Introduction

Now that we know how it is that we happen to be humans, the question before us is: how can the situation be corrected? Is there a way?

Yes, as a matter of fact, there is a way for both the already conditioned human being (those of us who are living now) and the beginner (those yet to be born). In order for each of us individually to benefit from the spiritual Truth of our being, we must become consciously aware of It by having access to It.

Chapter 7

For Those Who Missed the Way: The Spiritual Path Is the Way of Regeneration

For all who are now well-seasoned (conditioned states of Consciousness — humans), it is necessary to make a *conscious contact* with our true, real Self — make a *conscious contact* with Spirit. This will not be an easy, quick task. Why? Because in essence it means we will have to endure the extinguishing of all that we have come to falsely believe about who and what we are.

This false belief is the only thing standing in the way of our conscious awareness. It's like a cloud that blocks the rays of the sun from reaching the earth. The sun is probably the most potent of all natural forces. It is a major source of regenerative life to all living things. What's more, it is always, even though not visible to sight, being what it is — the sun. But its awesome brilliance can at times be completely blocked by some windswept, meandering clouds. This does not disturb us the least because we know from experience that the sun has not been permanently obliterated, just momentarily obstructed, and in time it will reappear.

Consciousness, the singular, creative Principle of the universe and of our individual world in particular, is omnipresent just like the sun. Our being unaware of Its omnipresence does not change Its nature; however, it does indeed affect our individual world or life experience.

Since Spirit/Consciousness, individual Consciousness, is *One*, if anything is occupying It except Truth, then whatever it is must first be removed, like the cloud that blocks the sun, in order that the Truth may be consciously known.

It will take commitment, devotion, effort, time, and above all, a wholehearted, earnest desire from each individual one of us. Note this carefully—each of us individually must do it for ourself. Even so, it isn't something that you or I can make a human choice to do; rather, it's something that has to develop in us. We cannot humanly conjure it up. We cannot humanly produce it. The earnest desire for it to be so has to evolve within us as our Consciousness gradually is prepared for that experience.

It comes of its own accord to those who have lived this human way of life—for many previous incarnations—to the extent that they have been unable to find any sense of permanent satisfaction in whatever they have humanly accomplished in life. Possessions, income, family, home—none has been totally satisfying for any great length of time. They have satisfied temporarily but not permanently, and that is what we are looking for—permanent fulfillment or satisfaction. This can only come from attaining *conscious union* with our real Self, which is infinite, whole, and complete.

We ourselves are infinite. But we have been shut off from conscious access to our infinite nature, and while we remain shut off, we will never be permanently fulfilled. How can you fulfill that which is infinite with something of a finite, changeable, material nature? It cannot be done! The only way you and I can fulfill our infinite nature is to find and establish our oneness with that *Infinite Invisible* — true Identity — which we already are.

You and I are already infinite — possessing all. However, at this stage and not knowing this, coming only into the intellectual awareness of it won't make it a reality to us. Something more is needed — we need to come into an *actual realization* of our true identity, and at this particular stage (seasoned humanhood) the only way that can happen is through our effort in making this inner *conscious contact*.

The way that I found to make this inner *conscious contact*, through my own experience, is by living morning, noon, and night with that which I call *The Question*: What is God? And the only way that you and I will be able to live morning, noon, and night with that question is by having a burning desire, a hunger and thirst, to have an answer to it. We want to make sure, however, that we are not allowing the mind to answer *The Question*. We want to ask *The Question* and then *listen* expectantly. Some kind

75

of response will eventually come to us, whether as a voice speaking, a feeling, or simply an awareness now of a Presence that we were not aware of before.

The response will not be instantaneous. As a matter of fact, it could take months or years. But if we are earnest, our persistence and perseverance will prevail, and some sort of response will unfold. We must have an *actual experience*—the conscious awareness of an unfolding or revealing *Something* communing with us from within our own being.

We develop ourselves to this point through the practice of meditation. Meditation is where we develop *the ability* to do *inward listening*. It is into the Stillness—Silence—within ourselves that we must listen, for it is out of this that *the still, small Voice* will utter Itself in response to our inquiry: *What is God?*

Since nothing manmade has adequately revealed Truth to us in a way that has left It unquestionable, we therefore have to turn within ourselves and trust what the saints, seers, and mystics of all ages have revealed to us: the kingdom of God is within us, and God is infinite wisdom—Omniscience—therefore, we must allow It to identify Itself to us. *We can go nowhere on the spiritual path without making this contact, a conscious contact.*

It must be understood that we are always in contact with our true identity; we just aren't conscious of that contact. We do not know of this contact from firsthand experience, and this is what we need. *This is what we need!* Whenever we can get ourselves quiet, when the thinking mind is stilled and we are listening, we are in contact with our true identity, in spite of the fact that It has not yet come into our conscious awareness.

We must practice this over and over again, morning, noon, and night. We take every opportunity to get quiet and listen within ourselves as we ask *The Question*: What is God? What is God? and we listen. With the practice of meditation, after a while we become almost naturally quiet within, and therefore we can carry *The Question*—What is God?—around with us during all of our waking hours.

The spiritual journey is the experience that each of us has to undergo within our own Consciousness as a result of not having had the benefit of an opportunity which only exists at conception: the opportunity of having our eyes shielded from the material scene until we are sufficiently developed to be able to hear the still, small Voice within utter Itself—identify Itself as "*I AM*." This occurs sometime during the first 36 months of every individual's life. Failing to have that opportunity, as a result of ignorance on the part of materia medica and family, it is the exposure of our pure Consciousness to the material world that ultimately causes us to come to believe ourselves to be the material human beings that we seem to be.

The spiritual journey upon which each of us is embarked is a journey in Consciousness back to Its original state—that state of pure, undefiled Consciousness that each one of us *is* now and always has been. It's just that this true state of our existence has been obscured. The journey in Consciousness that each one of us must now take—having missed out on the opportunity of being protected from the influence of material appearances—is the long, extended return or retracing of our human steps. It is *first* a shedding of this human state of Consciousness because it is *only* as we get rid of that which has been accepted in Consciousness—the false belief in a sense of self separate and apart from the one Divine Consciousness—that our true nature or identity can be revealed to us.

Consciousness itself is *One*. It can only be in one state! If It is in a false material state, then the false state must first be removed in order for the true spiritual state to be consciously known. Once it has been removed, we will then be in our original, pure, undefiled state of Consciousness. We will be in Spiritual Consciousness. Most importantly, we will be *consciously* in Spiritual Consciousness.

We are Spiritual Consciousness all along, but having previously accepted this false belief in a material sense of existence, we have no access to It; we have no knowledge of It. And we will never have access to or knowledge of It until this false state of Consciousness—this false belief that has been accepted—is sufficiently removed or dissolved to the point where the Light of Spirit can enter our conscious awareness.

This human state of Consciousness does not have
to be totally eliminated by us. We simply need to
bring our human state of Consciousness to the point
where It is humble enough to admit that It can't
resolve our problems in this human state of life. It
must come to yield Its ego, yield Its sense of "I can
do this or that thing"—yield to the possibility of
there being something within us that has to be the
resolution, be the difference, be the change in what
we have experienced thus far.

Pure Consciousness is exposed to this world, the
material/physical scene, before having access to the
still, small Voice, which is the Spiritual Interpreter of
all that Consciousness is aware of. The awareness of
nothing but materiality at this most impressionable
time—prior to having access to the still, small Voice—
becomes the basis, or foundation, of the material state
of Consciousness that is created. Because regardless
of whether it's true or false, whatever Consciousness
is aware of will in due time become accepted as the
state of Reality. Thereafter, when the individual
attains Self-awareness as "*I*," that "*I*" will interpret
Itself in terms of the nature of the state of Reality—
material or spiritual—that has already been accepted
as the individual's Being.

Chapter 8

Meditation Is a Necessity

For those of us who now have to travel the spiritual journey, I am reminded that each time we come to a state of silence within ourselves, we have made another step forward on the way. Each time that we consciously initiate the silence, no matter how many moments it lasts, we are on the way.

One external experience in this modern day that reminds me of the inner journey is a ride aboard a metro train or subway. A trip on the metro train to a destination entails many stops. As we stay on the train, this symbolizes our moving steadily ahead in stillness, and if we remain on the train, we will reach our destination without effort. But if we get off the train at each and every stop along the way, we are prolonging our journey. Moreover, if we remain at each one of these stops for any length of time, just that much longer are we prolonging our journey.

So, too, on the spiritual path. If we meditate incorrectly or fail to meditate at all, we are doing nothing but prolonging our journey. In the degree that we reach these periods of silence in meditation and are able to remain there for however long—moments or minutes—then we are steadily on the way. But we can't stay in this silence for any great length of time in the beginning.

As we continue to meditate, we find that it becomes easier for us to remain in the silence. The periods of inner silence we experience seem to expand, and as they do, we delight in them and want to experience them more often. This expansion increases until at some point, as a result of all the stillness we attain in our meditation, we do arrive at our destination of making a conscious contact with our true spiritual Self.

It is through meditation that we will ultimately be able to free ourselves from the imprisonment of the belief of a material sense of the universe. What is maintaining and sustaining this belief is the law of our individual Consciousness that causes us to unwittingly give it our attention. If somehow we can take our attention away from this mistaken belief, it will gradually dissolve because our attention—our individual Consciousness—is the only thing that sustains its existence. We are Spirit and Spirit is Life, so we are that which gives the false belief its existence. Take that away and it has to eventually disappear.

This is what happens when we meditate. We consciously decide to focus our attention on spiritual Truth—on God, the nature of God, the nature of man, and the nature of prayer. In doing so as often as we can, we are signaling the dissolution of that belief that had its foundation in the world of appearances, the world of nothingness, and since it has no law of its own to sustain it, it is not reality and it must dissolve.

The world of reality is spiritual—incorporeal, invisible, eternal, and changeless. What we are doing in meditation is conscientiously devoting our attention, our conscious awareness—our life, really—to Spirit and the things of Spirit. Anything in our Consciousness not of this nature and claiming an existence of its own is doomed.

Today there are many forms of meditation, but the method that brought forth the message of The Infinite Way, through Joel Goldsmith, is the one we must become familiar with. More importantly, we must become experienced in its proper practice.

Before we begin, it is extremely important that we find some quiet location where we won't be interrupted and the body is comfortable.

In addition, we will need to keep the eyes closed. Many students engage in meditation with the eyes open. This is all right, once we have become adept in the practice, but in the beginning and up until we have made a conscious contact with Spirit, it is best to close the eyes. It is to be remembered that our whole human dilemma stems from the fact that from the very beginning we, individual Consciousness, have been conditioned by appearances. This conditioning happened as a result of our eyes being opened, which resulted in our Consciousness being exposed to appearances. So now you and I, in our practice of meditation, must avoid the reactions to external appearances, which come automatically with the eyes open, by closing the eyes.

Meditation primarily consists of two very distinct sections, or aspects: contemplation and silence. The raw material, or ingredients, of the beginning contemplative aspect of meditation is the letter of truth, which we learn from The Infinite Way writings. Our intellectual grasp of the principles in these writings is what we are to use in this beginning stage of our meditation. By rehearsing in our mind what we know of some specific aspect of a principle relative to a particular problem that has been brought to our attention, we are deliberately redirecting our thought away from the patient, the student, and the problem.

We continue pondering — mentally rehearsing — the letter of truth, the principle we have learned, all the while being open to the spontaneous inflow of other thoughts directly related to it. These may very well be scriptural passages or just some random new slants on the principle. This is to be continued until such time as there are no more thoughts or ideas and we find ourselves to be mentally emptied — silent.

Here we have reached the second aspect, or phase, of our meditation. This really is when the actual meditation begins; this is the most important part. This is what we have been leading up to, this moment of absolute inner Silence. Here we take a *Listening Attitude* whereby we simply sit, listening into that Silence as if expecting to hear a voice or to become aware of "something." We do this effortlessly for a brief period. Then, when we sense that we are trying to sustain the listening, we stop. We have finished this session of meditation.

Through the continual day and night practice of meditation, we are establishing an *unconscious contact* with the Spirit within us. This contact will remain unconscious to us until we have practiced enough to sufficiently prepare our Consciousness so that It may open to receive the Spirit. Also, continuing to practice meditation develops our ability to do *inward listening*. It will be through this type of listening, if persisted in by practicing meditation, that we ultimately will be able to *hear* that oh-so-gentle still, small voice of Spirit at the center of our being.

Chapter 9

Our True Self Must Be Experienced

Understanding what happened in our Consciousness, how we became separated in the very beginning before we were even self-conscious, will make it somewhat easier for us to grasp the reason why we now need the contact with the Presence of Spirit within us. Since we know nothing about the invisible spiritual realm, the Presence, once consciously contacted, will be able with our cooperation, of course, to gradually lead us back to the center of our being where we can consciously reestablish our spiritual foundation of oneness.

There is a reason I keep mentioning that we are to *consciously* do this, that, or the other. In our true spiritual identity, we are already infinite, already one. But as separated human beings, we are not consciously aware of our true spiritual identity, and it is this conscious awareness that we are in need of.

What is God? We must make a *conscious* contact with Spirit. This contact must be a conscious encounter—an actual, known experience to us, within us. For it is after we have made this contact that we can go further. We can evolve—our Consciousness can evolve—as we learn to listen more and more, get quiet and be aware of this conscious contact we have made within. This is the way those of us who have gone well along the path of human living have to proceed at this stage. We have missed out on the most important facet/aspect of the spiritual life because of the ignorance of those who raised us. They are not to be judged or condemned, however, because they came into their legacy of ignorance quite innocently; it was the normal outcome of being raised by others who likewise were unaware.

Spiritual ignorance has been the major factor in the determination of where we are today in our development. It is because of that ignorance that we who have found our way onto the spiritual path now have to back up; we have to reverse; we have to retrace our steps, and in doing this, we find that we are "dying to" —that is, learning the truth about— much of what we have come to erroneously believe to be our real life.

Once we have made the inner contact—whether it takes a month, a year, or 10 years—from that point on, we will march steadily ahead in evolution toward that state of Consciousness which we have always been—*Oneness*. But it will be a gradual, evolutionary process, and as it unfolds/reveals, we will see more and more of that horizon, that *Oneness*. Once it has fully unfolded, we will then be in that state of having a *realized* state of spiritual Consciousness—a *realized* state of being, a *realized* state of awareness of the truth of our identity. From this illumined perspective, we will be able to look back and actually see how we got to be where we are right now and why it took so long.

One of the first things we will see is all the years that were spent developing to that stage in life where we found ourselves totally dissatisfied with life as a human being. This encompassed the years leading up to our mid-30s to early 40s and sometimes later. Very few of us have progressed to the point where we are totally dissatisfied with our human sense of life in less than that time frame. There are some who have been led to the spiritual life at an earlier state, but they have not come onto the spiritual path for the sake of Spirit itself. They have come onto the spiritual path because they have felt it to be a way to obtain something from Spirit, something of a human, material nature that would satisfy their need at the moment.

By and large, most serious seekers led to the spiritual path have spent many years walking in life seeking out those things that seemed to satisfy a human being, only to learn that they really didn't provide the satisfaction they thought they would or that the satisfaction they provided did not last very long and they found themselves wanting again.

Even after those 36 to 40-plus years and we find ourselves led to the spiritual path, it still takes quite a number of years afterwards to bring ourselves into *realization*. There are the 40 years in the wilderness after we have discovered the spiritual life. In those 40 years, we find ourselves making contact then losing it; struggling to regain it and maintain it within; then finally *realizing* It—that is, becoming consciously one with It. Where there is no longer an "It" and a "me," there is only It—*One*. This is the ultimate—Spirit/God/Consciousness—*All*—*Oneness*.

Interestingly enough, as we do develop/evolve into this realized state of *Oneness*, which finds us endowed with spiritual discernment and spiritual vision, we are able to look back and understand that if *this one thing* had happened in our earliest days, all of these years of struggle to find what we have at long last come to discover about our true identity could have been avoided.

Chapter 10

For Coming Generations: The Opportunity to Retain the Conscious Awareness of the Gift of Spirit

For future generations, there is an untried approach, at least to my knowledge, that will assure the establishment of the spiritual state of Consciousness from the very beginning. It will be of much shorter duration (the short way) than the common spiritual journey (the long way) that must be taken by each one of us who lost the opportunity to experience this approach due to its being available only to, and effective in, the newborn child.

So what is this approach? It's simple, really, but at the same time virtually unthinkable to us as humans. Without a doubt, it will be more difficult for young mothers and fathers to adopt than for anyone else. Then, too, there is materia medica, which will also need to cooperate.

This, then, is what needs to occur universally in every newborn: the eyes must be completely shielded from all visible appearances until that portion of the brain—the prefrontal cortex, the *seat of Consciousness*—is sufficiently developed to allow access to the *still, small Voice* that utters the word *"I."* When the word *"I"* is heard, the eyes can be freed to view the world.

The effect of having all material appearances obscured from sight for perhaps 24 to 36 months will be the protection of the pure, spiritual state of individual Consciousness. Being so shielded, individual Consciousness will not be allowed the opportunity to develop a belief in (1) a material sense of the body and of the universe, (2) some things being good and some not so good (evil), and most importantly (3) a personal, separated sense of self.

With these evidences of an accepted human state of Consciousness no longer posing an obstruction, pure Divine Consciousness—the individual Consciousness of all—will then have exclusive, conscious access to the awareness of Its own spiritual Truth. Spiritual Consciousness will then be the nature of individual Consciousness, and along with Its faculties of spiritual vision and spiritual discernment, It will be the foundation and anchor of the individual's life. In this state, *Oneness* will be the nature of *Reality*, just as in the world's present human/material state of Consciousness, *separation* is the norm.

If only our parents had been aware of the *profound consequences to our conscious development* that would result from the simple act of *opening our eyes* without having access to spiritual Truth. Had they known this, they would also have known to *cover/shield our eyes from this outer world of appearances* until such time as we became aware of the *still, small Voice,* the "*I AM,*" within us. In other words, until sufficient development had taken place in our brain that would permit this "*I*" to voice Itself directly in our conscious awareness.

If our eyes could have been shielded from all appearances up until that time, we would have been blessed because when we did open our eyes, we would have heard within ourself this "*I AM.*" It would have identified Itself as "*I.*" And when It said "*I,*" It would not have been referring to any one particular thing or person. It would have been *recognizing Itself* by proclaiming Its own identity, "*I AM,*" in regard to everything It became aware of — with no exceptions. In other words, Its recognition would have been all-inclusive — universal.

Once our eyes are permitted to view appearances, Consciousness instantaneously begins Its function of creating — causing to come into existence. What Consciousness will very soon create, or cause to be, in this early stage, is the individual's perception — belief — of Reality in whatever It is aware of. Since, at this point, Consciousness is only aware of material/physical appearances, It will create the individual's Reality — yours and mine — out of those appearances. It will create a material sense of the universe because It has been exposed to nothing but appearances.

However, if from day one our eyes are shielded from all appearances, we will be aware only of the invisible in which there is complete harmony, complete purity. We will hear, taste, and touch things, but these will have considerably less impact upon our Consciousness than witnessing them (actually seeing with the eyesight).

And if for a certain period of time—24 to 36 months—our vision is shielded from all material things, Consciousness will not create a reality out of those material things. It will not create a material sense of existence but will remain pure, undefiled, for It will not be the least bit aware of any material forms—instead, only the invisible. When that period of time—24 to 36 months—has elapsed and the eyes are uncovered, in answer to every question and in response to every appearance, the still, small Voice will say, "*I AM.*"

I sense jaws dropping in astonishment that some-one could have the nerve to even suggest that new parents wait almost three years before having their first look into their precious little one's eyes. I know! I know! Believe me, I realize what an almost impossible expectation this is. Three years! Have you lost your mind?

But consider this: if this approach is not taken, human life as we know it now will continue unchanged, and *future generations will have us to blame* for the many predicaments that will befall them; the law of Consciousness will assure it. No manner of exterior improvements in lifestyle and standard of living will change life as we now know it. So long as mankind functions from a Consciousness of separation, there will be warfare, inharmony, lack, man's inhumanity to his fellow man in some form or degree, which will manifest in and as the life experience in general. Only when there is a changed Consciousness, one that is no longer human or material in nature but is spiritual, will there be everlasting peace and brotherliness among all peoples of the world.

The above-mentioned approach is a way to hasten the day when this will be a reality rather than what it is to you now as you first read this—the outlandish suggestion of one who loves his fellow man enough to be willing to share this inwardly revealed truth. Suffice it to say that if something different, even something radical, isn't either proven to be true or disproved as ridiculous, then be prepared for more of the same human life experience being generated by an unchanged state of Consciousness.

To put this three-year period in perspective, consider this: for those of us living now, including any new arrivals as this is written, researchers have established that in general it takes *36 to 40-plus years* before an individual is even ready to be turned in the direction of the spiritual journey (see in particular *Cosmic Consciousness* by Dr. Maurice Bucke). Look at the world now and see just how few there are of the four billion people on earth who are led to the spiritual way of life.

In addition, from my own personal experience I have learned that it takes almost the same length of time, after having made the initial, inner conscious contact, to come to the state of *realization*. Now, I ask you, if there were any possible way to do in 36 months what it is now taking the very few who are led to the path roughly 70 years to accomplish, wouldn't you be willing to save future generations this ordeal?

Chapter 11

Original Perfection:
Invisible Formlessness—Oneness

A separated, personal sense of self can never develop if Consciousness remains pure and free of belief in anything other than the spiritual Truth. From the very beginning, it is the exposure of our pure individual Consciousness (causative/creative Principle) to nothing but the world of material appearances that causes our individual Consciousness to create a perception of reality—the belief—in a material sense of existence. The exposure and its effect happen in the months before individual you and I have become consciously aware of ourselves as "I."

Ensuring that individual Consciousness stays free of any awareness of material form during the earliest months of existence, by finding some way to shield the physical eyesight for a certain period of time, is the only known way that this can be made effective.

Even with the eyes closed, Consciousness is still conscious. Being conscious is Its nature; hence, never is It anything but conscious. Consciousness is never unconscious! When the physical body is asleep and it seems our human self is unconscious, actually we are not, since our true Self is Consciousness and It is continuously maintaining all that constitutes the activities of the body—the beating of the heart, the circulating of the blood, breathing, and so forth.

Consciousness is always conscious by way of the avenues of awareness—the senses. In their original, pure state, the senses are spiritual in nature. They are the means by which we become aware of our world. Vision (spiritual or physical) is the most significant and influential of the senses. Whatever the senses are aware of—spirituality or materiality—is the determinant of the ultimate "state" of our individual Consciousness.

At birth and thereafter, in the early months of our existence when we are totally unaware of our spiritual identity—our true Self, the *"I"*—and have no access to Its spiritual nature and attributes, our individual Consciousness is nevertheless constantly and continuously aware (conscious) of only that to which the senses are exposing It. Because there is no access to the spiritual Self and Its faculty of spiritually discerning Omniscience (Truth) during this most impressionable period, all that remains is "this world"—the world of material appearances. This, a material sense of the world and everything in it, including ourselves, then becomes the foundation of the perception of reality—the belief—which is *created* by Consciousness. Acting on this belief, mind *forms* concepts, which are expressed as the manifest world of individual you and me.

In Its pure, spiritual state, Consciousness will produce perfection, completeness, and wholeness, which is the reflection of Its own formless, invisible nature. It will continue to do this as long as nothing interferes with or interrupts Its flowing forth in the entirety of Its pure, spiritual state. However, let something stand in Its way as a blockage or an obstruction of some sort, and then the quality and nature of what It reflects changes.

In each of Its own individualizations as man, there is a limited physical body provided for the purpose of individual expression on the material level of existence. Consciousness functions through the instrumentality of this physical form. That is, the physical body is an instrument of Consciousness.

Now, this would be fine if this instrument, the physical body, were as fully developed as is Consciousness—but it isn't. *This is where the obstruction or blockage originates.* The *entirety* of the nature of Consciousness is not permitted access into the instrument (the limited physical form) in the very moment the individual is born. The crucial aspect of the nature of Consciousness that is *absent* at that most significant time is *spiritual Truth*, the still, small Voice, which is the source of spiritual interpretation, spiritual vision, and spiritual discernment.

From the very beginning, individual man has no access to this all-important facet—the eternal, changeless, spiritual Truth—of his own spiritual identity. This Truth constitutes the reality of Being, and if from the exact point that It enters the individual's conscious awareness nothing else has been permitted to enter beforehand, It will negate any other succeeding claim, thereby rendering it to be nothing. Consequently, in the absence of spiritual Truth, whatever Consciousness becomes aware of can only be a falsehood—error. However, since Consciousness has no way of distinguishing the Truth from error, whatever It is constantly exposed to will become accepted as the reality in the experience of the individual and will create the corresponding external effects.

This predicament will continue for all those who are being born until it becomes known, until we become aware of this experience and how to deal with it. It can be dealt with. It won't be easy, though. It isn't something that you and I will be at all comfortable with because it is radical. Nevertheless, radical though it may be, this is what is necessary in order for there to be some change.

It should be obvious to the world by now that none of the traditional human modes of knowledge and experience have produced much in the way of lifting mankind out of its dilemma—humanhood. A lot has been done in the area of improving mankind's standard of living but little or nothing to enhance its quality of life.

The Truth is forever true, changeless, invisible, and real. It is the most essential facet of Being. If you and I and all of mankind are unaware of Its existence, that does not affect Truth—it affects us!

The one omnipresent, all-powerful, all-intelligent Source that is maintaining and sustaining this entire universe in its perfection and completion is also that which sustains and maintains us. But from the very beginning, we as individuals are totally unaware of this, and this state of unawareness is what is now sustaining the problem.

This creative Principle and Power not only creates, maintains, and sustains all we know to be this universe but also performs that function in and as our individual life experience, and because It is limited to an awareness of only material appearances, It creates our reality out of those appearances.

We come to accept what we see with our physical eyes as the reality of being because the one creative Principle within us, our Consciousness, having accepted a false belief, has created that reality. It has created that reality because It has not been made aware of Its own Truth in Its individual manifestation as you and me, as a result of the voice of Truth being unable to become an active and alive facet of our conscious awareness as yet—*as yet* meaning in the earliest months of our coming into this world.

We are in this world for many, many months before we become consciously aware of our self, of our own individuality. Consciousness, however, is in full operation in us, and by the time (24 to 36 months) we do become consciously aware of our individuality, the previous exposure of Consciousness to nothing but material appearances *has already created* a false material sense of reality in us.

The false, universal belief is not something hanging out in space someplace, waiting for us to be born and hypnotized by it. No, the false belief is created at the same point in time and in the same way in each of us individually, without exception, and that is what makes it universal. All of us undergo, or have undergone, the same identical experience. The few exceptions that do eventually come happen later on in life when certain individuals—having in previous lifetimes consciously developed to the point of realizing the futility of the human sense of life—arrive at that place where they begin to turn away from their humanhood in search of some other meaning for being here, for having been born. These few are looking for something that gives them a permanent sense of peace, joy, harmony, and fulfillment. Since they have not been able to find this in their human lives and have exhausted all their intellectual know-how, they are forced to become humble, having no other recourse but to turn within themselves to seek some answer(s) there.

We can never be spiritually fulfilled as long as there is a sense of some lack. The most profound lack that we all have is the lack of an understanding of our own true nature, our true identity. This primal lack will be the cause of our failure to find permanent contentment in any other department of our lives. When we have attained, through inner revelation, the answers to all the questions we have concerning our true nature—*and have attained the realized experience of those answers*—we will then find that we are totally fulfilled, having achieved that peace which passes understanding.

The following excerpt is from Joel Goldsmith's Infinite Way *Letter* of May 1965 and relates to the length of time it takes a student to rise high enough in Consciousness to do healing work—and this, mind you, with the original teacher and revelator—available, alive and in person (italics mine):

There are many more individuals seeking a spiritual solution to life than there are persons prepared to help them find that way. Even today in The Infinite Way, we are unable to take care of the many demands that come in asking for spiritual help. It would be sad if the world turned to us now, and we have to say, "We are sorry. We know this truth is the answer, but our students have not attained a high enough state of consciousness to give that spiritual help.

After seventeen years? How long does it take? How long does it take a student to attain spiritual consciousness? I can give you half the answer. A student cannot even begin to attain that consciousness until his goal is no longer that of meeting his personal problems of health, supply, or happiness. He must no longer be preoccupied with personal gain. *The search for God-awareness must become the primary motive of study.* When that is true, then the spiritual student is halfway "home." He must decide that the attainment of Christ-consciousness is his only goal and that having help for his other problems is of secondary importance. I am not saying that anyone should neglect human situations or obligations, but these should be secondary. It then might not take a student too long.

What, then, is the prospect of attaining spiritual Consciousness for those of us who have no such immediate contact? Consciousness is the one creative/causative Principle, individualized as the Consciousness of man. Our Consciousness, then, is that which *creates/causes* our world. What our Consciousness creates or causes is belief—a perception of reality—from which the mind *forms* a concept.

The universal creative Principle, Consciousness, though individually expressed as man, is nonetheless infinite in Its individualizations and forever maintains and sustains Its creation. In individual man—the image and likeness of the creative Principle, Consciousness—life is expressed in a unique way, as the experience of each of us is likewise unique. The degree of harmony each of us exhibits will depend on the state of our Consciousness.

Originally our Consciousness is absolutely pure, and if left to Itself, It would be the source of perfection, wholeness, and fulfillment. In this state, we would know nothing but joy, love, peace, and brotherliness among mankind all over the world. Here we would be aware only of Consciousness—God, Spirit, *"I AM"*—made individually manifest wherever we happened to look. There would be no sense of separation, and without this, there would be no cause for discord. Each individual would be *anchored* spiritually in Divine Love. This would be the feeling experienced while in the presence of another person, regardless of where we might find ourselves.

However, since an observance of the present, as well as a look at the past, reveals that we are living in a different type of world and having a different type of relationship with one another, it is obvious that something has interfered with the unfoldment of Consciousness when It individualizes as man.

In addition to our own infinite, individual Consciousness, we possess a finite, physical form that is insufficiently developed at birth. This condition of the physical body becomes an *influence* that prevents, obstructs, or blocks the access of individual Consciousness to Its own Truth of Being.

First, mankind has not yet realized that Consciousness is forever being what It is—conscious. It never ceases being conscious. So when It individualizes as you and I, It is fully conscious—fully functioning— despite the fact that at this time (at birth and quite a few months thereafter) you and I are not individually aware of It. The reason is that during this time period we are not yet *self-aware*—that is, our physical form has not developed to the point where the still, small Voice can make Itself known in us by uttering Its identity, "*I AM*," which in truth is our real identity.

The opened eyes of the individual automatically and instantaneously initiate in Consciousness the creation of the perception of reality—the belief—in whatever It is constantly, consciously aware of. These beliefs then become the foundation upon which our individual life experience is constructed. Consciousness (your individual Consciousness and mine) is absolutely impersonal, neutral. Therefore, regardless of the nature of that to which It is exposed—the Truth or the absence of Truth (error)—our Consciousness will see to it that this becomes what we believe to be reality, the truth, in our individual experience.

The Truth of Being, if originally accepted as reality, would result in spiritual discernment accompanying any presentation to the eyes, rendering vision spiritual in nature and capable of seeing through material appearances rather than the restricted physical eyesight, which can see only the material appearances. But having no access to the Truth of Being, our individual Consciousness begins creating the foundation of our life experience, our perception of reality, by being exposed to nothing but material/physical appearances. This quickly, normally and naturally, results in the acceptance of a material sense of the universe and of life itself.

The attraction and attachment to human comfort and ease will continue to foster the obscurity of the true reality of Being. As humans, we won't be able to easily loose ourselves from these enticements, and this will result in prolonging the day when we will even consider attempting to discover our true nature.

Human gratification in worldly things will see to it that we remain in "this world."

This is the reason why expecting any real change in mankind as a whole does not look at all promising anytime in the foreseeable future. However, before we conclude that the spiritual journey is a hopeless endeavor, there yet remains the potential for mankind—if mankind becomes aware of it and, more importantly, takes the step of acting to bring that potentiality into reality. Since nothing we have attempted thus far has taken us or the world very far along on the spiritual journey, that is reason enough to explore some as yet untried approach.

A telling revelation dashed in upon me not too long ago: if this false, human, physical, material sense of a world, with all its inharmony, discord, and inhumanity to man, is the product of man's individual Consciousness being constantly, consciously exposed universally to external appearances, then the antidote, or solution, would have to be the diversion of individual Consciousness away from material appearances, depicting separation, to the realm of the invisible, or spiritual, where all is One.

Essentially what this means, for all of us presently walking the face of the globe, is that we must spend more time behind closed eyes while we are active in meditation. We must make a regular practice of getting still—silent—and take many, many opportunities during both day and night to turn within to our invisible spiritual center, to be receptive *(listen)* to whatever may unfold or reveal itself from within us.

About the Author

John Drewery is a teacher and practitioner of the spiritual message of The Infinite Way, as revealed by Joel S. Goldsmith.

John was born and grew up in Virginia and spent his early adult years living in metropolitan Washington D.C. In 1978, during a period of "deep darkness" and emptiness, he was led to make a trip to California. While there, he came across Joel's work. Joel's message brought an inner peace, and he felt "Something" leading and guiding him.

"As the weeks turned to months, then years, the heavy door to the dungeon of human Consciousness was cracked open just a bit, and in a flash, some light, a new realm of awareness, dawned ... I stepped foot on the spiritual path, never to turn away again."

John makes his home in Southern California. He publishes a monthly letter entitled *Whispers from Within* and is available to give classes.

More information is available on his website: www.instillness.com.

www.ingramcontent.com/pod-product-compliance
Lightning Source LLC
Chambersburg PA
CBHW051817040426
42446CB00007B/718